SUN BEARS

by Tammy Gagne

AMICUS HIGH INTEREST   AMICUS INK

Amicus High Interest and Amicus Ink
are imprints of Amicus
P.O. Box 1329, Mankato, MN 56002
www.amicuspublishing.us

Library of Congress Cataloging-in-Publication Data

Gagne, Tammy, author.
 Sun bears / by Tammy Gagne.
    pages cm. -- (Wild bears)
 "Amicus High Interest is published by Amicus."
 Summary: "Presents information about the sun bears of Southeast
Asia, their rain forest habitats, and their climbing skills."-- Provided by
publisher.
 Audience: K to grade 3
 Includes bibliographical references and index.
 ISBN 978-1-60753-779-3 (library binding)
 ISBN 978-1-60753-878-3 (ebook)
 ISBN 978-1-68152-030-8 (paperback)
 1. Sun bear--Juvenile literature. [1. Bears.] I. Title.
 QL737.C27G327 2015
 599.78--dc23
                       2014043619

Photo Credits: Andras Deak/iStock/Thinkstock, cover; Dane Jorgensen/
Shutterstock Images, 2, 4–5, 13, 14–15, 22, 23; Molly Marshall/Shutterstock
Images, 6; Joe Blossom/Alamy, 9; Sohns/ImageBrokerRM/Glow Images,
10; ZSSD/Minden Pictures/Corbis, 16–17; Clemens Bilan/AFP/Getty
Images, 18; Fabio Lamanna/Shutterstock Images, 20–21

Produced for Amicus by The Peterson Publishing Company
and Red Line Editorial.

Designer Becky Daum
Printed in Malaysia

HC 10 9 8 7 6 5 4 3 2 1
PB 10 9 8 7 6 5 4 3 2 1

TABLE OF CONTENTS

HERE COMES THE SUN BEAR

Sun bears are found in Southeast Asia. They live in **rain forests**. Sun bears mainly stay high in tree branches.

5

SMALL FOR A BEAR

Sun bears are the smallest kind of bear. They grow up to 5 feet (1.5 m) long. Their chests have golden fur. They are named for this fur. It sometimes looks like the sun.

Fun Fact

Each bear has its own chest fur pattern.

CLIMBING HIGH

Sun bears are good climbers. Long claws help them grab trees. Strong legs help them climb. The bears rest and eat up high in trees.

Fun Fact
Sun bear claws can be 4 inches (10 cm) long.

FINDING FOOD

Sun bears sniff to find food. They smell insects hidden in trees. They dig out the bugs with their claws.

A SWEET DIET

Sun bears also eat fruit. Another food they like is honey. They lick honey out of beehives.

Fun Fact
Sun bear tongues can be 10 inches (25 cm) long.

TWIST AND DEFEND

Sun bears have loose skin. This helps keep them safe. Tigers or large snakes grab sun bears. The bears can twist around. They can then bite the **predator**.

BABY BEARS

Most kinds of bears have two cubs. Sun bears usually have just one at a time. Mothers can give birth at any time of year.

RAISING CUBS

The mother raises the tiny cub. She keeps it safe. The young bear is **mature** by age four.

Fun Fact

Mothers sometimes walk upright. They hold their cubs like human babies.

SHRINKING HABITAT

Sun bears are in danger. People take over land where they live. Their **habitat** shrinks. Some people hunt sun bears. New laws protect sun bears from hunters.

SUN BEAR FACTS

Size: 59–143 pounds (27–65 kg), 48–60 inches (120–150 cm)

Range: Southeast Asia

Habitat: rain forests

Number of babies: 1

Food: insects, fruit, honey

WORDS TO KNOW

habitat – a place where a plant or animal naturally lives

mature – fully grown

predator – an animal that hunts another animal

rain forests – places with lots of trees, heavy rainfall, and many plants and animals

LEARN MORE

Books

Brown, Gary. *The Bear Almanac*. Guilford, Conn.: Lyons Press, 2009.

Dolson, Sylvia. *Bear-ology: Fascinating Bear Facts, Tales & Trivia*. Masonville, Colo.: PixyJack Press, 2009.

Editors of TIME for Kids and Nicole Iorio. *Bears!* New York: Harper Collins, 2005.

Websites

San Diego Zoo—Sun Bear
http://animals.sandiegozoo.org/animals/sun-bear
Find more fun facts about sun bears.

World Wildlife Federation—Sun Bear
http://wwf.panda.org/about_our_earth/species/profiles/mammals/sun_bear
Learn more about where sun bears live and the dangers they face.

INDEX